~ The Jesse Tree ~
28 Family Devotions
For Advent

By Anna Sklar

The Jesse Tree—28 Family Devotions for Advent

Copyright © 2016 by Anna Sklar

ISBN-13: 978-1537572055
ISBN-10: 1537572059

Books may be purchased online:

Createspace.com

Amazon sites worldwide

Digital Downloads available on Etsy:

https://www.etsy.com/ca/shop/SklarInk

Contact the author at:

Simply Live Blog—*annasklar.ca*

Etsy Shop—*SklarInk—etsy.com/ca/shop/SklarInk*

To All the Families
Who Celebrate Advent Together

Praying the Shema for Your Family:
Based on Deuteronomy 6:5-9

Let these commandments be on the hearts of our family. Impress them on our children. May we talk about them when we sit at home and when we are out in the world, when we lie down and when we get up. Teach us to tie them as symbols on our hands and bind them on our foreheads. Help us to write them on the doorframes of our houses and on our gates. Fill us with a desire to grow spiritually and impress Your word into the lives of our children. I give our family to You believing that Your plans for us are far beyond what I could ever hope for.
In Jesus' Name, Amen

Introduction

What Is Advent?

The word "Advent" means coming. The fourth Sunday before Christmas marks the beginning of Advent season. Advent is a time of waiting - for Christmas and for the coming of Jesus to our world. During Advent, we prepare our hearts and our homes to celebrate the birth of the Messiah.

What Is A Jesse Tree?

"A shoot will come up from the stump of Jesse;
from his roots a Branch will bear fruit."
~ Isaiah 11:1 ~

Jesse was the grandson of Ruth and Boaz. Jesse was the father of King David. The prophet Isaiah prophesied that a very special person would come from Jesse's family. This person was Jesus Christ, the Messiah. The Jesse Tree traces Jesus' lineage all the way back through the Old Testament. A collection of stories make up the Jesse Tree - stories of Jesus' family and Israelite history.

The Jesse Tree is a fun way to celebrate Advent with the children in your life. This books contains a set of 28 family devotions for you. Each devotion highlights a story of Jesus' lineage or Israelite history, a scripture reference to read, a discussion idea and a prayer reading.

How To Use The Jesse Tree Family Devotions

On the first Sunday of Advent, read the story in the Jesse Tree book labelled *Creation.* Children can turn to the scripture passage in their Bible if they are old enough. Discuss the question(s) in the *Talk About* section and read the prayer with the children. Do this every day during the Advent season, in numerical order, finishing up on Christmas morning with the devotion labelled *Jesus Is Born!*

You can also encourage the children to lead the Jesse Tree devotions with your family.

Table of Contents

1. Creation   **Read:** Genesis 1-2:3

Before there was anything else, there was God. He wanted to create our world, and the first thing He made was light. He called the light Day and He called the darkness Night. Next God made Sky, Ocean, and Land. He told plants and trees to start growing from the earth. Then God told the sun to shine in the day and the moon and stars to shine at night. Ocean creatures and birds came next, then animals and reptiles. The last thing God created was humans. He let the first man - Adam - give names to all the animals and birds. Adam also named his wife, Eve. When God finished making our whole world He looked at it and said all of it was very good. Then He made a special time of rest for our world. He also took a rest Himself because He had finished His work. Whew!

Talk About: What is your favourite thing that God made in our world?

Prayer: Thank You God for making our world and for making us. Help us to take care of everything in the world the way You want us to.

2. First Sin   **Read:** Genesis 2:15-17 & 3:1-6

God made a beautiful garden called Eden. It was Adam and Eve's job to take care of the garden. Eden had all kinds of delicious fruit trees in it. Two special trees were in the middle of the garden. One gave life that lasts forever and the other gave power to know what is right and what is wrong. God told Adam and Eve not to eat from the tree that gives power to know right and wrong, but they could eat from any other trees. There was a snake living in the garden - it was really the devil in disguise. One day the snake tried to trick Eve into eating the fruit from the one tree they were supposed to leave alone. Eve chose to eat the fruit even though she knew she wasn't supposed to. Adam didn't try to stop her and then he chose to eat the fruit too. God knew what happened and He was very sad. He had to tell Adam and Eve to leave the beautiful garden. They couldn't enjoy the fruit trees or walk and talk with God in the garden anymore. God still loved Adam and Eve and still talked with them, but everything changed.

Talk About: Did you make a choice today that you are happy about? Did you make a choice that you are sad about?

Prayer: Lord, help me to make choices that make You happy. Forgive me when I make choices that make you sad. Thank You for always loving me, no matter what.

3. Flood and Rainbow   Read: Genesis 9:8-17

Adam and Eve had many children and grandchildren and great-grandchildren and great-great-grandchildren. Soon there was a lot of people on the earth. After a while the people stopped making good choices, and kept making only bad choices. God could only find one person on the whole earth that was making good choices and still loved God. That person was Noah. God decided to send a flood that would cover the whole earth and destroy almost everything, but He also decided to save Noah and his family. The animals and birds would be saved as well. God told Noah to build a huge boat called an ark and fill it with at least two of every kind of creature. Noah had the job of storing up enough food for his family and all the creatures in the ark. It took a long time to build the ark and gather the creatures and food, but Noah did the jobs God gave him. Noah's whole family was saved when the flood came. Rain poured down for 40 days and nights. Noah's family and all those creatures floated safely in the ark for about a year, until all the water dried up. God made a rainbow and made a promise to never flood the earth again.

Talk About: Why does God always keep His promises?

Prayer: Thank You, God, that we can trust You and that You never break Your promises.

4. Abraham   **Read:** Genesis 12:1-7, 15:5-7

There were many people on the earth again. God told one good man named Abram to leave his country and go to a place God would show him. Abram loved God and wanted to do as God asked, so that's exactly what he did. He took his wife Sarai, his nephew Lot, and all of his things with him. Abram left his home, his family, and his friends to follow God. He didn't even know where He was going! When they came to the land of Canaan, God made a promise to Abram. God said, "I will give this land to your family forever." There were other people living in Canaan at that time and Abram didn't have any children yet, but God would keep the promises He made to Abram when the time was right. God changed Abram's name to Abraham (that means *father of many people*) and told him that his family would have as many people in it as there are stars in the sky! God also promised to be the God of Abraham's family forever. Everyone on earth who believes in God is part of that family that God promised to Abraham.

Talk About: How many people are in your family? How many people do you think are in Abraham's family that God promised to him?

Prayer: Thank You, God, for my family that You gave me to live with, and thank You for my family of God that is so huge I can't even imagine.

5. Isaac   Read: Genesis 22:1-18

A special visitor came to Abraham's house one day. It was the Lord, who promised Sarah and Abraham that they would have a son in about one year. Sarah laughed because she was 90 years old and never had any children. She thought it was impossible, but nothing is impossible with God. They did have a son, just like God promised, and they named him Isaac. Abraham was 100 years old when Isaac was born. Many years later God gave Abraham a test to see if Abraham would obey him no matter what. God told Abraham to take Isaac up a mountain and offer him as a sacrifice. Abraham didn't understand why God was asking him to do this, but he always wanted to obey God. He trusted that God knew what He was doing. Abraham arrived at the mountain and got ready to do what God asked, even though it would mean hurting the son that God gave him. Suddenly Abraham heard an angel shout "Don't hurt the boy! Now I know you will always truly obey God." Then God provided a ram for the sacrifice instead of Isaac. God never wanted Abraham to hurt his son at all; He just wanted to see if Abraham would trust Him and obey him no matter what.

Talk About: When was a time when it was hard to do what God asked you to do?

Prayer: God, help us to do what You ask us to do, and thank You for blessing us when we obey You.

6. Jacob

Read: Genesis 28:10-15

Isaac and his wife, Rebekah, had twin sons named Jacob and Esau. The oldest son was Esau and he was born just before Jacob. In those days, oldest sons got to keep all the land and animals that belonged to their father when their father died. Jacob wanted all his father's things for himself, so he tricked his father Isaac and his brother Esau into giving them to him. Esau was very angry and planned to kill Jacob after their father died. Jacob had to run away from home to escape from Esau's anger. Jacob went to his uncle's house to live there until Esau's anger settled down. That might take a long time! Jacob laid down to rest one night during his long journey to his uncle's house. As Jacob slept he had a dream. In his dream he saw a ladder that reached from earth to heaven. Angels were going up and down on the ladder, and the Lord stood above it. God told Jacob He would give him and his future family all the land around him. God said Jacob's family would be too big to count and they would be blessed. Then God promised to be with Jacob and watch over him always.

Talk About: Have you ever tricked someone? How? Isaac promised to give his belongings to Jacob even though he was tricked. Do you think Isaac's promise to Jacob will come true? Promises are very important!

Prayer: Lord, help me to only make good promises that I can keep.

13

7. Joseph   **Read:** Genesis 37

Jacob got married when he was living in his uncle Laban's home. Jacob had 12 sons, and Joseph was his favourite. Joseph was given a very special coat of many colours from his father, and this made all the other brothers angry. Joseph had a dream that all his brothers bowed down to him and this made the brothers even more angry! They made a plan to hurt Joseph but they sold him to be a slave instead. Joseph was a slave to a leader in Egypt and he went through many hard times, but God was always with Joseph. God was always watching out for Joseph. One day Joseph became second-in-command of all the Egyptians and helped the whole land when there was not enough food for everyone. Even his brothers came from far away to find food. They didn't recognize Joseph when they asked him for food. They actually bowed down to him because he was an Egyptian ruler. So Joseph's dream came true after all. He forgave his brothers, and took care of them, and gave them lots of food.

Talk About: Why is it important to forgive others when they hurt you or do something wrong to you?

Prayer: Thank You Lord, for forgiving us. Help us to forgive each other and to remember you are always with us.

8. Jacob's Blessing On Judah

Read: Genesis 49: 8-12

Pharaoh promised Joseph's brothers that he would give them the best homes and land in Egypt if they came and lived there. When the brothers told their father Jacob that Joseph was still alive, he was so happy! The whole family left their home in Canaan to go live with Joseph in Egypt. God spoke to Jacob as he was travelling to Egypt and told him, "Don't be afraid to go to Egypt because I am with you. Your family will be a great nation there." When Joseph saw his father again he hugged him and cried tears of joy. Pharaoh was happy to meet Joseph's family and give them the best land he could find for them. Jacob gave Pharaoh a blessing. Jacob (also called Israel now) blessed all his 12 sons before he died. He gave a special blessing to his son Judah - that someone in his family would one day be a leader over all the others. Do you think the blessing was about Jesus? Jesus wouldn't be born for hundreds of years yet, but this is one of the first promises of His coming to us. Jesus is sometimes called the *Lion of Judah*.

Talk About: Why was Pharaoh so nice to Joseph's father and all his brothers?

Prayer: Thank You for always taking care of us and for always bringing good things into our lives, even if there are some bad things as well.

9. Moses

Read: Exodus 3:1-10

The Israelite families got bigger and bigger. The new king of Egypt didn't know about Joseph or how he helped Egypt during a very hard time. He didn't know that the Israelites were Joseph's family and they were supposed to be friends with the Egyptians. The new king was scared that the Israelites would take over the country! So he made the Israelites into slaves and he was very mean to them. One baby boy, Moses, was hidden by his mother so he wouldn't get hurt. She hid Moses in a basket on the river and Pharaoh's daughter found him. The princess took care of Moses like he was her own son. When he was grown up, Moses knew he was really an Israelite. He got very mad one day when an Egyptian was hurting one of the Israelite slaves. Moses killed the Egyptian and then Pharaoh wanted to kill him! Moses ran away from home and went to live in the desert. He married a shepherd girl and he had children and he was happy. One day God spoke to Moses from a bush that looked like it was burning. He told Moses it was time to free the Israelite slaves and God wanted Moses to tell that to Pharaoh. Moses was scared, but he went back to Egypt to free the Israelites.

Talk About: Why was the new king of Egypt afraid of the Israelites?

Prayer: Thank You God, that you are always there to help us when we are scared.

16

10. The 10 Commandments

Read: Exodus 20:1-17

Moses travelled back to Egypt with his family and told Pharaoh to let the Israelite slaves go free. Pharaoh said no. God gave Moses special skills and tools to show His great power to Pharaoh. But Pharaoh still wouldn't let the Israelites go free. After Moses caused many bad things to happen to Pharaoh and all the Egyptians, Pharaoh finally let the Israelites go. They weren't slaves anymore, they were free! They started travelling away from Egypt and all of a sudden Pharaoh changed his mind about letting the Israelites go free. Pharaoh's army chased after the Israelites to bring them back to slavery. Moses used God's power to make the Red Sea spread apart so the Israelites could walk through safely, away from Pharaoh. Then the water crashed back down on Pharaoh and his army. A while later, God gave the 10 Commandments to the Israelites. This was a list of ten of the best ways to live. The 10 Commandments said things like make sure God is the most important thing in your life, have a day of rest every week, listen to your parents, don't kill or steal or lie, and be happy with what you have.

Talk About: Do you have a list of rules to follow in your house? How do the rules help your family?

Prayer: Help us to follow the rules even when it's hard, so we can love each other better.

11. Rahab   Read: Joshua 2: 2-21

After God used Moses to free the Israelites from slavery, they set out to live in Canaan, the land God had promised them a long time ago. Many other people lived in Canaan, so they had to fight lots of battles to get the land. The first battle they fought was for a city called Jericho. The leader of the Israelites was now a man named Joshua, because Moses had died. Joshua sent two spies into Jericho to figure out the best way to capture it. There was a kind woman named Rahab who lived in Jericho. She helped the Israelites defeat the city. Rahab hid the spies in her home so they wouldn't be found or get hurt. The Israelites promised to keep Rahab and her whole family safe when it was time to capture the city. They told her to tie a red rope up in her window and they would come get her and keep all her family safe. They kept their promise to Rahab and she lived with the Israelites after Jericho was destroyed.

Talk About: How will God help the Israelites get the land He promised to them?

Prayer: Lord, sometimes it is so hard to wait for something we really want. Help us to be patient when we have to wait for Your promises to come true.

12. Gideon

Read: Judges 6:36-40

The Israelites sometimes had a hard time following God and doing what He asked them to do, even after winning many battles and seeing many miracles from God. Sometimes God would let them be slaves again for a little while so they would ask Him for help and follow Him again. One time God chose a man named Gideon to free the Israelites from the Midianites. Gideon was the smallest in his family and his family was from the weakest tribe, but God saw Gideon as a mighty warrior and wanted to use Gideon in big and powerful ways. Gideon asked for signs from God to see if he was hearing God correctly when He asked Gideon to do something. Gideon put some wool on the ground and asked God to make it wet and keep the land around it dry – God did that. Then Gideon asked God to keep the wool dry and make the land around it wet – God did that too. Now Gideon knew He was really hearing God correctly when God asked him to free the Israelites from slavery. God did amazing things through Gideon, like defeating a whole army with only 300 men. After the Israelites were free they lived in peace for the rest of Gideon's life, which was about 40 years.

Talk About: How can God use you to do mighty things for Him?

Prayer: Show me what You want me to do for You, God, and help me if I feel too scared to do it.

13. Ruth and Boaz   Read: Ruth 1:16-17

An Israelite man took his wife, Naomi, and their two sons to live in a land outside of Canaan. There was no food around their old home in Bethlehem. They found food in Moab and they lived there a long time. The two sons grew up and married women from Moab - one woman was named Ruth. Naomi's husband and two sons died in Moab and Naomi decided to go back home to Bethlehem. Ruth decided to go with Naomi because she wanted to stay with her. She told Naomi, "Where you go I will go, and where you stay I will stay. Your people will be my people and your God my God." In Bethlehem, Ruth found some barley for them to eat in a field. The owner of the field said she could take the barley. His name was Boaz and he was a good man. He said he would marry Ruth and take care of Naomi for the rest of her life. Ruth and Boaz had children and grandchildren and great-grandchildren. Jesus came from their family many, many years later. And you know who Boaz's mother was? Rahab - the lady who helped the Israelites defeat Jericho. Jesus' family is made up of some very interesting people!

Talk About: What happens when we are kind to one another?

Prayer: Thank You, God, for giving us chances to be kind to others and thank You for being kind to us.

14. Jesse and David   Read: 1 Samuel 16:1-13

Remember that Jacob gave a special blessing to Judah before he died - that someone in his family would one day be leader over all the others? Well, we've been reading all about Judah's family. Rahab married an Israelite man from Judah's family. Rahab was Boaz's mother. Boaz married Ruth. Boaz and Ruth had a grandchild named Jesse. That's where the name *Jesse Tree* comes from. In Isaiah 11:1 the Bible says, "A shoot will come up from the stump of Jesse" and then it talks about a very important person who will be born into Jesse's family one day. It all starts with Jesse's son, David. David was a shepherd who fought lions, loved to play the harp, and most of all loved God. The Israelite people really wanted a king to rule over them. The first king was Saul, but he was not very good at following God, so God chose another man to be king. Can you guess who it was? It was David. David went through many hard times, and he didn't always make good choices, but he loved God so much and he was a good king for the Israelites. God made part of the promise to Judah come true through David being king. And God made a special promise to David that someone from his family would have a kingdom that lasts forever.

Talk About: Who was Jesse's grandmother and grandfather? Who was Jesse's son?

Prayer: Thank You, God, for the Jesse Tree and learning the history of the Israelites.

15. Elijah   **Read:** 1 Kings 18:16-39

There were many kings that ruled the Israelites after David. One of David's sons built a beautiful temple (like a church) for the Israelites, but most of the kings of Israel were not nice men. Most of them stopped following God and even started praying to statues and other things they pretended were gods. They forgot there is only One True God and this made God very sad and sometimes very angry. God did so much for His people but they just kept forgetting about Him. One day God gave a man named Elijah a special job. Elijah was a prophet (a person who gave the Israelites messages from God and tried to remind them to keep following God). The job Elijah had was to gather 450 prophets of a fake god named Baal and meet them on Mount Carmel. He told the prophets of Baal to ask Baal to send fire to an altar they set up. An altar is a place where they worshipped gods. The prophets of Baal tried and tried but no fire came to the Baal altar. Then Elijah asked God to send fire to the altar he had set up for God. Elijah only had to ask once and God sent a great fire to His altar. All the people remembered God and followed Him again.

Talk About: If God was a super-hero, what powers would He have? Who could defeat Him?

Prayer: You are the biggest, strongest, most powerful super-hero of all time and I'm glad I follow You!

16. Hezekiah

Read: 2 Kings 18:5-8

One of King David's sons, Solomon, became king after David died. He was a good king at first and built a beautiful temple in a city called Jerusalem. But later on he made a lot of bad choices and didn't follow God very well. God allowed the Israelites to split apart into two kingdoms - Israel and Judah. Both kingdoms did things that were evil and God was not happy with His people at all. Once in a while one of the kings would be good and choose to follow God. Hezekiah was one of those good kings. He was a king of Judah. The Bible even says, "There was no one like him among all the kings of Judah." Soon after Hezekiah became king of Judah, the kingdom of Israel was destroyed by the Assyrians and the people of Israel became prisoners. And when Hezekiah was king of Judah, all but one of his cities was taken over by the Assyrians too. The only city left was Jerusalem. Hezekiah prayed to God and asked God for help. God remembered a promise He made to king David a long time before. He promised that Jerusalem would be a special city and its temple would be a special temple for the Israelites. God sent an angel to defeat the enemies. The angel killed 185,000 enemies in their tents one night, and then the enemy stopped attacking. Jerusalem was safe for a long time after that!

Talk About: Why did the Israelites make so many bad choices?

Prayer: Thank You for loving us, no matter what.

23

17. Josiah   Read: 2 Kings 22:1-2 & 23:1-3

Hezekiah's son, grandson and great-grandson were all kings of Judah at different times. And they all made bad choices and didn't follow God. Then Josiah became king - when he was only 8 years old! After he ruled for 18 years he wanted to make some repairs to the temple in Jerusalem. As they were fixing the temple, a special scroll was found. It was called the Book of the Law and it had the first parts of the Bible written on it. The scroll talked about creation, the flood, Moses, the 10 Commandments and much more. When king Josiah read the Book of the Law he was very sad because he knew that God's people were not following Him. He made the best choice just then. He got rid of everything in his kingdom that helped people follow fake gods and he told everyone to start following that One True God again. God was so happy with Josiah and all he did to help his people follow God again. The Bible says, "Neither before nor after Josiah was there a king like him who turned to the Lord as he did - with all his heart and with all his soul and with all his strength."

Talk About: Why was God happy with King Josiah?

Prayer: Lord, help us to remind people about You and help them to follow You.

18. Isaiah Talks About The Prince Of Peace

Read: Isaiah 9:6-7, 11:1-5, 10-11

Josiah's son and grandson were kings of Judah after Josiah died, but they did not follow God. God was tired of His people making bad choices and the kings choosing fake gods instead of the One True God. So God let all the Israelites be captured by their enemies and the cities of Israel were all destroyed. But just a minute - there is still hope for God's people! When Hezekiah was king there was a prophet named Isaiah. He prayed to God a lot and God gave Isaiah messages to share with the people. One night Isaiah had an amazing dream. In the dream he was in heaven and he saw the Lord on His throne and angels around Him. And in another dream God gave Isaiah a very special message for the people. He told Isaiah that one day a child would be born from David's family and this child would bring peace to the people. This child would be called things like Prince of Peace, Wonderful Counsellor, Mighty God and Everlasting Father. Isaiah's message must have been very good news to the people!

Think About: Who was the child Isaiah was talking about? What does Prince of Peace mean?

Prayer: Thank You for the child, God; thank You for Jesus.

19. Israelites Become Prisoners

Read: Jeremiah 11:7-8, 31: 31-34

God made a promise to Abraham and all his family that He would always be their God. He promised that things would go well for them if they chose to follow Him. But we've learned that for hundreds of years the Israelite kings didn't listen to God and didn't follow God. Once in a while a king would love God and help the people follow God again. Then after a few years the Israelites would start following false gods again. God was getting fed up so He let the enemies of the Israelites capture them and all their land, including the city of Jerusalem. Jerusalem was a special city to God and the Israelites because it's where the king lived and where people would worship God together during holidays. But the enemies of the Israelites destroyed all the cities of the kingdom of Israel and took the people as prisoners. Then the Israelite enemies destroyed all the cities of the kingdom of Judah. Jerusalem was the last city to be destroyed. This must have been a very sad time for God and all the Israelites. But God promised the prophet Jeremiah that one day He would rescue the Israelites from their enemies and once again they would love Him and follow Him.

Talk About: How do you feel when others don't listen to you?

Prayer: Help us to hear and follow You always, Lord.

20. Israelites Rebuild Jerusalem

Read: Ezra 1:1-3, Nehemiah 2:17-18

The Israelites had another name - they were also called the Jews. After their enemies destroyed all their cities, the Jews were allowed to stay in Jerusalem and rebuild the city and live there. Enemy guards stayed and watched over the Jews. God changed the heart of the enemy king, and more and more Jews were allowed to return to Jerusalem for the special job of rebuilding the temple. The Jewish people began to follow God again and do the things He asked them to do. God was keeping his promise to Jeremiah. A few years after the temple was rebuilt, the Jews were allowed to rebuild the walls around the city of Jerusalem. When the Jews were finished rebuilding the temple and the walls, the city once again looked like the special place God wanted it to be. The Jews were still ruled by kings who were not Israelites. Sometimes the kings were nice to the Jewish people and sometimes they weren't. God had made a lot of promises to send someone to save His people. The Jews waited and watched for a few hundred years before Jesus was born. We'll read all about His birth in the next few days.

Talk About: Did God still love the Jewish people, even when they were prisoners? How do you know?

Prayer: God, thank You for all the chances You give us, and for always loving us.

21. Zechariah

Many different kings ruled over the Israelites after they rebuilt the temple and the walls of Jerusalem. Mostly the kings still let the Jews follow God and live in peace. Once there was a priest named Zechariah and he loved God very much. He was an older man, and he and his wife weren't able to have children, even though they prayed and asked God for children. Zechariah was praying in the temple one day and an angel appeared to him and said, "Do not be afraid, Zechariah; your prayer has been heard. Your wife Elizabeth will [have] a son, and you are to call him John." The angel also said that John would be a great follower of God and people would want to follow God too because of John. One other important thing the angel said to Zechariah was that his son John would get the people ready for the coming of the Lord - the special person the Israelites had been waiting for! Remember how hard it was for Abraham to believe he would have a son in his old age? Well, Zechariah didn't believe the angel at first, so he wasn't allowed to speak until John was born. When people asked Zechariah which name to give his son, he had to write it down! As soon as he did, he could speak again.

Talk About: Have you ever had trouble believing something in the Bible?

Prayer: Thank You, God, that you never lie and we can believe everything we read in Your book, the Bible.

22. John The Baptist   Read: Luke 1:18-25, 57-58

The name of the angel who appeared to Zechariah in the temple was Gabriel. The angel was right about the baby, and everyone was so happy when Zechariah and Elizabeth had the son that Gabriel said would be born. In those days, oldest sons were usually named after their fathers. When it was time for Zechariah to name his son, he knew he would have to tell people the baby's name was John - just like Gabriel said. Zechariah still couldn't speak, so when everyone asked him what name to give the baby, he wrote out the name John. Suddenly Zechariah could speak again. The first thing he did was praise God! John must have been a special baby to have all this happen in his family's life. People wondered what he would be when he grew up. John was actually Jesus' cousin and he grew up to be a special prophet who told the Jews about the coming of Jesus. John baptized many people and sometimes used a scallop shell to pour the baptism water.

Talk About: What happened to Zechariah when he didn't believe what Gabriel said?

Prayer: Thank You God for the special people You give us in our lives to help us know more about You.

23. Mary

Read: Luke 1:26-38

God had another job for the angel Gabriel. Another special baby was going to be born - the most special baby of all time! Gabriel must have loved these two jobs of telling people about the babies they were going to have and how important those babies were going to be in the world. This time God sent Gabriel to talk to a young woman named Mary. Mary was going to be married to a man named Joseph, but they weren't married yet. Gabriel said to Mary, "Don't be afraid. God is very happy with you. You will have a baby boy and you must call him Jesus. He will be God's son and He will be King over the Jews. He will have a special kind of kingdom that never ends." Gabriel also told Mary that her cousin, Elizabeth, was going to have a baby even though Elizabeth was very old. The angel told Mary that nothing is impossible with God. Mary agreed to do whatever God wanted her to do. She had a very good and pure heart.

Talk About: What do you think it's like to talk with an angel? How do you think Mary felt about the news from Gabriel?

Prayer: Thank You that we don't have to be afraid of the jobs You give us to do.

24. Joseph

Read: Matthew 1:18-25

Mary had promised to become Joseph's wife. Joseph came from a special family. Remember the blessing on the tribe of Judah - that someone would come from that family who would rule over all the others? Well, King David came from Judah's family. Remember how God told Isaiah that someone from David's family would come and bring peace to the Jewish people and He would be called things like Prince of Peace, Mighty God and Everlasting Father? Well, guess who came from King David's family... It was Joseph. And who do you think God wanted Joseph to be a father to here on earth... it was baby Jesus! So baby Jesus was part of Joseph's family, who was part of King David's family, who was part of Judah's family. God kept all the promises we've been reading about in the Jesse Tree stories. When Joseph found out that Mary was pregnant, he didn't know if he should still marry her. But an angel came to visit Joseph to tell him God still wanted Joseph to be Mary's husband, and a father to Jesus, God's Son. Joseph was a carpenter and he built things from wood. He taught Jesus how to be a carpenter too.

Talk About: Who was Jesus' father on earth? And which family did that earthly father come from?

Prayer: It is really amazing, God, how You work out Your plans on this earth.

25. Shepherds — **Read:** Luke 2:8-20

It was getting close to the time when Jesus was to be born. He had been growing big and strong inside Mary. Joseph and Mary were married now. The Roman king named Herod told everyone to travel back to the towns where they were born because he wanted to count how many people were in his kingdom. So Joseph and Mary had to travel from their home in Nazareth to the city where Joseph had been born - Bethlehem. Joseph and Mary went to Bethlehem just as Jesus was ready to be born. It's almost Christmas, isn't it? Now, there were some shepherds in the fields around Bethlehem and they were taking care of their sheep at night. God sent an angel to talk to the shepherds (most people think the angel was Gabriel) and tell them about the birth of Jesus. The angel told the shepherds where they could find Jesus and then many angels appeared and praised God together. When the angels left to go back to heaven, the shepherds decided to go see baby Jesus. They were very excited!

Talk About: How did the shepherds feel when they saw the angels? What do angels do?

Prayer: Thank You God for sending us Your angels sometimes to help us in our lives.

32

26. Star and Magi   Read: Matthew 2:1-12

There were many people who were waiting for the special person who was supposed to be born into the family of Jesse. It had been more than 400 years since the walls and the temple of Jerusalem were rebuilt. That's a long time to wait! There were some wise men called Magi and they learned that the birth of a special person was coming soon. Who was that special person? It was Jesus. The Magi travelled a very far distance to come see the baby Jesus and bring Him gifts of gold, frankincense, and myrrh. They followed a bright star in the sky on their journey. On their way to see Jesus, King Herod found out about the Magi's visit and he asked them where they were going and what they were doing. Herod was scared because he didn't want someone else to become king. The Jewish people thought the special person that was coming would be king instead of Herod, and free them from the Romans. But Jesus wasn't born to be that kind of king. He was King of the Jews in a way that freed everyone from their sin and bad choices. He came to save everyone from God's punishment for their sin, not free them from the Roman king.

Talk About: The Magi gave Jesus 3 gifts - what were they? What's the best Christmas present you ever got?

Prayer: Thank You for Jesus - the best gift ever.

27. Manger

Read: Luke 2:1-7

At the time of Jesus' birth, there were a lot of people travelling. The shepherds were coming to see Jesus, the Magi were coming to see Jesus, and even Jesus was travelling while he was growing inside Mary. Joseph and Mary had to travel to Bethlehem - do you remember why? There were so many people travelling around that when Joseph and Mary got to Bethlehem, there was nowhere for them to stay! There was no hotel rooms and even no room in people's houses. Joseph really needed a place for Mary to rest because baby Jesus was going to be born very soon. One person finally let Joseph and Mary rest in a barn. What is usually in a barn? Animals, straw and maybe a stinky smell! It would have been nice and warm, though. And maybe the straw was comfortable to rest on. I hope they brought blankets for Mary to lie down on while Jesus was being born. They got a manger ready for Jesus to sleep in after He was born. A manger is like a big wooden box for holding the animal's food and water.

Talk About: Where were you born? Was it anything like a barn with a manger?

Prayer: Thank You, Jesus, for all the travelling You did for us - all the way from heaven to earth.

28. Jesus is Born!   Read: John 1:1-5, 10-14

We've been waiting for this special day to come and it's finally here! Imagine how long the Israelites waited for their special person to be born from the family of Jesse and David, who were from the family of Judah. Think about all the people in Jesus' family that God made promises to - did He keep all His promises? Is Abraham's family too big to count? Did the Israelites live in Canaan? Was a special person born from Jesse's family? Yes, God kept all the promises He made to His special people. He can't help but keep His promises. He can never make a bad choice because He can never sin. Even though there are bad things happening in our world all the time, this was not God's choice for us. Way back in the Garden of Eden, and with the Israelites, and on into our world every day, we have a hard time choosing to follow God sometimes. So the earth and the people in it are living in a world that is not perfect. But God promises to turn the bad stuff that happens into good. Jesus was the best thing that happened in our world. He made it so we can be in heaven with God one day. Happy Birthday, Jesus!

Talk About: Do you believe Jesus was God's Son and that He came to free people from sin? Do you want to be free? Ask someone to pray for freedom with you.

Prayer: Jesus - I believe in You. I want to be free from all my sin and live with You in heaven one day. Amen.

About the Author

Anna has been celebrating Advent with her family since her first year of marriage.

Her husband made her a wooden Advent candle holder that still graces their home every Christmas season.

Through the years, her sons would light a candle when they read one of these Jesse Tree stories.

Anna loves to make easy-to-use resources for the family that encourage a more simple life and a chance to truly live in the moments of each day.

She enjoys life in Northern Ontario with her husband & two growing sons.

Anna loves to read, write, weave, quilt, bake, walk, and bicycle.

More From Anna

Simply Live Blog—*annasklar.ca*

Etsy Shop—SklarInk—*etsy.com/ca/shop/SklarInk*

Other Resources by Anna

The Jesse Tree Series (2016):
28 Family Devotions for Advent
28 Colouring Pages with Stories for Advent
28 Ornaments for Advent with Family Devotions
& Images to Colour
Lunchbox LOL Series (2016):
200 Jokes for the Lunchbox
200 Silly Questions for the Lunchbox
200 Days of Word Play for the Lunchbox
200 Calculator Word Games for the Lunchbox
200 Fun Facts & Trivia for the Lunchbox
200 Riddles for the Lunchbox
200 Holiday Jokes
Complete Lunchbox LOL Series

The Princess of Dreams (2016) - a children's story

Thy Word—A Journal of Reading Through the Bible in a Year (2014)

Discovering Hope—Sharing the Journey of Healing After Miscarriage, Stillbirth or Infant Loss (2013)

Coming Soon

The Jesus Tree—48 Family Devotions for Lent (2017)

Thy Word—My Journal of Reading Through the Bible in a Year (to be published annually starting in 2017) - a daily reading & blank journal